# Now, Now

**PITT POETRY SERIES**

Ed Ochester, Editor

# *Now, Now*

Jennifer Maier

UNIVERSITY OF PITTSBURGH PRESS

Published by the University of Pittsburgh Press, Pittsburgh, Pa., 15260
Copyright © 2013, Jennifer Maier
Manufactured in the United States of America
Printed on acid-free paper
10 9 8 7 6 5 4 3 2 1
ISBN 13: 978-0-8229-6263-2
ISBN 10: 0-8229-6263-2

*For my mother*

*and for Ralph and Virginia Wedgwood*

*Time (t) = distance (d) / velocity (v)*

*"It's a poor sort of memory that only works backwards,"*
*the Queen remarked.*

—Lewis Carroll, *Through the Looking Glass*

# Contents

# One

## HANGMAN

First, a box for the scaffold. Next a pole, hooked,
where the noose will go. Then seven spaces underneath,

like the broken centerline the father will cross when he feels
under the seat for the bottle, because it is a long way to town,

the road a running scar through the dense woods, and you
watching hard in the dark like he tells you for something

that might run out, suicidal. *Ready* you call, and he says *E,*
like you knew he would, and you make a circle, happy

for this word without an *e* and because the father is the best
driver in the world, able to steer with just one knee,

or a thumb looped through the wheel. *R,* he says, *and T!*
and you mark these next to the head, like the first dumb

thoughts of a man with only a straight line for a body
and another for a leg, a man who will probably be dead soon,

or else missing something important—hands, maybe, or a nose—
something he needs to live. *Y* comes next, an odd choice

you think, so you ask *why Y?* and he says *because because,*
and you both laugh, washed in the headlights that slice

through the cab like a quick and painless incision, knowing,
one day, after you have a name for it, that this is joy—

tucked safe in the kerosene smell of bourbon that is the sweet,
sharp spoor of the father—how you know you could find him

if he were lost in these woods, the way animals know their own
kind, could save him with your amazing sense of smell.

*H-I-J-K!* he shouts, and you add ears because it looks bad
for the hanged man, the sad stick body and curving frown,

the way you will picture the father thirty years later, after
they find him and the coroner tells you not to look. *O* he says,

and there are two of these—not together as in *booze* or *doom*—
but separated, you know, by *l* and *c*, which, when you say it fast,

sounds like *luck luck*, what you wish now for the father who loves
to win, and for the condemned man, who might be innocent after all,

his fate hanging on the alphabet and on this word you've been saving
so long. *S* is for sorry, as in *Sorry there is no S*, and *F* is for fireball,

which happens in movies when they crash through the guardrail
and tumble down the canyon because the father is not at the wheel,

but some bank robber who gets what he deserves, and *A* is for the ashes
that are left, white and clean, dropping straight down through your hands

into the bay. *In the midst of life we are in death,* each in our little car,
driving through the long day and the long night till we get

where we're going. *G,* he says, quietly, lighting a cigarette, and because
you agreed on no fingers you hang a heart on the skinny chest, like a note

left on a pole, and he can still get it you know he can if he just concentrates,
so you hand him the bottle, taking the wheel as he leans back, eyes closed,

thinking. *N goddammit!* he says finally and you say *Yes, yes,* then silently,
like a prayer, *L is for lava that flows from the molten secret heart of the world,*

*down the mountain, toward the slumbering village.* Then stops. The way
the father stops dead—*Volcano!*—in the middle of the road, then peels off

grinning, the lights of the town coming into view, the man on the page
safe now, hanging by an eyebrow.

## Big Tree

If life is but a dream, and time, a collapsible cup,
then who's to say the stranger in the car next to yours—

smiling at the big tree you have strapped into the front seat
of your convertible as you drive home from the nursery—

was not, after all, the most felicitous of husbands,
better, even, than you'd dared to hope?

Simple enough to shift what might have been into what *was,*
to remember how you dug the hole together, lowered it

trunk and root, turning it like this, like this. That was when
you were just starting out, the way running straight and long

through the town where you lived; not yet the treacherous
curve; not yet the cross at the side of the road.

And how much a family car can hold! Detritus of decades
brimming from boxes, bleeding through paper bags,

your hand light on the wheel through the long drive
and the children asleep in the back, or singing *merrily, merrily,*

love, like breath, fogging the windows; small fingers
tracing their names. And if it all passed in an instant,

a comfort now to know you had your life of ordinary good,
of love's tart fruits, its showery blossoms.

And now he is gone, lost up ahead somewhere and you
won't see him again. But that, you recall,

was the deal you made when you smiled back: the past,
once yours, you wouldn't trade for any other,

ringed by the past you're living now—here,
beside the big tree, whose spreading arms will shade it.

## RESPONSIBLE PERSON

Isaiah has made a Responsible Person,
big as life, and pinned him to the wall
over his bed.

The teacher said, *It's you, but in the future,*
as she passed around the crayons,
the safety scissors.

That was when he was eight, and his father
still lived at home. The future, he knew,
just waited around

for you to get there, like your birthday,
or the fractions at the back of *Our Numerical World*—
"not a thing, a part of a thing."

We stand together at the door to his room,
Isaiah's father and I—not his mother,
the woman after his mother—

and study the Responsible Person.
Smiling, square-shouldered, with large brown
shoes, he looks, we agree, like someone

you could count on, one of the numbered
good on which the world depends, a man
secure in every part of himself,

with two paper legs strong enough to hold him,
each small tear repaired from the back,
so it doesn't show.

## PAPER ROSES

I am eleven. I have taken my mother's razor.
I want to be sexy but still good,
like Marie Osmond, who lives in Utah
and can get any boy she wants.
Somewhere at the back of the house
"Paper Roses" is playing on the radio.
I listen, one leg propped on the edge
of the sink, the other dotted with toilet paper—
white blossoms with small red centers—
and when it gets to the part where
Marie sings *O how real those roses seemed*
*to be*—I'm doing fine, driving long,
straight rows through the lather, thinking,
*I am a born shaver!* and then, *Why didn't she*
*notice that sooner?* And worse,
if Marie's love could turn out to be
*Only im-i-ta-tion-* . . . a big red rose made
of paper—then what chance did normal
people have? When love came to you,
long-stemmed and breathing out perfume,
how could you know that it was safe
to fall? Before you *had* fallen,
before it was too late for you?

Years go by, decades. I don't think
about Marie—why should I?
It's the future and I'm driving to my own

house, when the man on the radio says—
offhand, like he's not sure it's news—
that her son has leapt to his death
from a hotel window, and now
I am moving forward on the straight
black road, and now I am standing at the sink
with a razor in my hand, the days
falling everywhere around me like soft
red petals, as her voice, on key and wise
with youthful sorrow, questions how
it could have happened that way,
how love could do a thing like that.

## LOVE POEM

My brain is in love with your brain,
and my body is just nuts about your body.
My brain thinks your body is the *ne plus ultra*
of sinewy perfection. My body goes in awe
of your brain, a dim sibling, loping behind.
*And my heart?* My heart is a bloodhound
with two masters. It tracks you through
the deep woods, first this way, then that.
The body whistles; the mind blows its silver horn.

Soon we will find you, treed and waiting.
The mind will stand poised with its camera;
the body, raise its barreled scope. The heart
will run around and around in circles as they argue
about the future, and birds scatter like buckshot,
piercing the dawn with their little cries.

## DAPHNE TO HER FATHER, GOD OF RIVERS

After the sculpture *Apollo and Daphne* (based on Ovid's *Metamorphoses*), Gian Lorenzo Bernini, Galleria Borghese, Rome

*You ask for news at the end of my first season:*

> I used to fear the hot breath of the god, now
> only fire, mirrors. It is nearly complete,
>
> my hands a green immolation, my mouth
> a knot hole —No—No. An owl roosts
>
> at the crook of my neck. A kind of music,
> the shrieks of small, expiring things.
>
> The sun provides; I neither chew nor swallow.
> My skin is black as Africa.
>
> What are the days? Hours fall. I mark
> their alluvial traces.
>
> Spring is taking me from inside. Blossoms,
> pale, scentless, cover my rocky
>
> bed. I am thirsty. Come with your floods
> and know me completely.
>
> Erase the print of his sandal behind me.

## ETYMOLOGY

What kind of word is *overjoyed*?

The dour diagnosis of an over-saddened
doctor, or the confession of a shy woman,
unused to strong participles as unused to wine.

Each word a window, each a mirror.

See through the wavering glass a distant town.
See the man, a draft waiting to be filled,
and the woman, a smatter of unparsed tenses.

See your reflection, speaking their improbable future:

the sentence you, like God, compose for them:
*And their joy rose steadily in the time of their lives*
*until it breached the rim of each delicate vessel.*

## DAYDREAM WHILE FRYING BACON

Four strips, pink and white in the pan—
four lanky Depression kids
sharing a bed. Let them
have bacon for breakfast

and a mother who stands
with her back to the window,
fork poised in the air like
a question mark. And let

me be the woman next door
she doesn't approve of, who lives
alone and doesn't go to church.
Men come, bringing flowers

and go, whistling a tune.
Between our houses, a path
of trampled grass. I see
their clothes waving on the line,

one nation, indivisible; she sees
mine, lacy and too small. She
thinks, *These women of the future.*
All morning I sit at my desk,

my mind a hot iron, moving
backward and forward

over the sheet she has pinned
to the breeze, facing me.

At dusk she will carry it inside,
unfurl it over the mattress, and
tuck it securely in. So each
makes a bed—tight! sweet!—

for the thing she loves.
So the past finds us on the air,
the smell of bacon from
a neighbor's kitchen.

So the future stands with a fork,
an iron, a borrowed spade,
turning it over
with an invisible hand.

# JANE

We accepted the facts without question:
the pert daughter of a famed explorer,
who falls for the big jungle lunk. So what

if he couldn't talk? He was an ape-man
aristocrat and she, a blonde with a plan.
She cooked and managed his studies,

and mostly he rescued her—from Pygmies,
short men in blackface, or the fat python,
flicking its tongue in a tree as she swam

naked below, waiting to drop down on
her shoulders like a mink stole. We sat
cross-legged in our uniform skirts, marking

his slow evolution—Tarzan mouthing words
or using a comb—the way a woman shapes
a man, haft and point, into the thing she needs,

yet knowing, with something like instinct,
that while a boy raised by apes might be *unlikely,*
Jane was pure make believe: the good,

A-student girl who gives up everything
for sex. We imagined them doing it, not
in twin beds like Ricky and Lucy, or like our

parents, safe in the sanctioning dark,
but wild as hyenas, free as the great apes.
And if you were like her, dipped in the waters

of her nature, how could you find your way
home to that lost continent? How could
you ever return? By summer

we'd lost them, though I kept her in mind,
the distant cousin who'd welcome me,
should I arrive unbidden in the leafy foyer.

I saw her again the other day, still fetching
in her jungle frock, still running ahead of him
on a ridge. *How did you do it?* I called,

and she turned, swinging me a vine. *Follow me,
Sister,* she called back. *Climb on. Step off.
Open your mouth, and scream your heart out.*

## Heat and Light

Whatever it was in the novel *Ethan Frome*
that caused Sister Bertrand to assign it
to every sophomore English class
for three stolid decades
is no clearer to me now, rereading it
by firelight, in the middle
of my life.

She must have thought the subject
of doomed, illicit love
would slow the downward slide
she'd marked in faces streaked
with rouge, in pleated skirts,
rolled at the waist.

But even as a cautionary tale
it missed the mark. Starkfield,
the drear New England town
where Ethan lives with his cold wife
and Mattie, the hired girl he loves,

was nothing like Seattle,
where it hardly ever snowed.
And if each felt herself to be,
like them, thwarted by circumstance,
hostage to the clanking radiator,
the gray, relentless rain,
it was nothing like Sister,

trapped in her drab habit forever.
The trees we glimpsed through steam-clouded
windows were not the dire beacons
of Wharton's novel. Not yet.

As for the protagonists, dim Ethan
and Mattie, with her portentous
crimson scarf, what did we care
that their passion smolders like
damp kindling through the first
ninety-seven pages? Love,
our true religion, would save them
in the end.

That it didn't was our fate, too,
matchless until then,
and I am here to testify,
late witness at the site
of an old injury:

*There was a sled*
resting like an unlit pyre,
and two lovers, broken for good,
and, in the white wreckage
of a winter hour,
the girl I was, rising from her desk

to ask, *Why didn't they just take poison*
*or throw themselves under a train—*
*something reliable?*

as the others nodded their assent,
and our teacher, turning from the window,
replied, *More heat than light,*
and we copied it down
for the test.

# Two

## NEW YEAR'S EVE

Now that the giant ball is poised for its descent,
and we're waiting for the final countdown,
why not reflect, in the time we have left,

on the wisdom of welcoming the birth
of a New Year that may, after all, prove
our last. Wouldn't it make more sense

to mourn together the too-quick demise
of one that's seen us safely here, to a friend's
living room, steadied by the pelf and store

that survived his prosperous forbears:
the gilt mirror that frames our happy party,
or the tall clock, whose pendulum swung

through each grandfather's final hour,
in a year that began like ours,
with an earnest toast to his good health?

But why should we mourn, you ask—
the big orb half way down—
when the Future, clean and pressed,

and with a bit of sparkle, awaits only the form
each will supply to make it hers alone,
and when the few seconds that remain

of the past is long enough to watch the bubbles
rise in each slender glass, and to feel ourselves
held light and golden in Time's mouth,

before the great ball rests, and the cheer
goes up, and the sweet, sad hymn
for old times' sake begins.

## YOUR LIFE IN DANCES

One day you will not recall the Tango.
The quick trail of the Foxtrot will have gone
cold—stepped out for good with the Twist,
the Hustle, and the Boogaloo.

Then, from your seat by the window,
your life in dances may seem nothing more
than the repetition of a single question
asked and answered in a score

of forgotten languages, in some gilded
ballroom or louche lounge, or in the open air
under swaying branches. On that day,
you may think the sun, warming your face

through the glass, an agreeable festoon,
or the mirrored orb that shone down
on the party like a god's eye, witness
to each tenuous first step, each turn

and counter turn, and the little slide
that left you somewhere else—
alone at the punch bowl, or smiling
into the face of a stranger—as the beat,

slow and sure, or wild as a faltering pulse,
went on and on, alive and voiced

as the brown-suited crooner on the window
sill, at whose invitation the soul

rises, now, from the stiff chair of the body
and steps once more and light as breath
toward the whirling center, all
strange light and startling music.

# FLY

... —and then it was
There interposed a Fly—

—#465, Emily Dickinson


I had no wish to interpose—
I kept my distance on the windowpane.
The room was hot and close.

She lay in white, expectant as a bride. Repose
became her. While mourners prayed in vain
I watched the sky; I never interpose.

In fact, I'd just as soon be elsewhere when it goes.
The green world's fresh with corpses—why remain?
I wanted out. The room was hot and close.

Bright birds get poems; I'm lucky to get prose.
What's that to me? Patient, I circle round. Your Bane's,
my Inspiration, my blank page. Why *should* I interpose?

The *Amherst Journal* struck me, I suppose.
And stunned, I stumbled, reeling on the windowpane.
The air was blue; the room was hot and close.

She might have heard me buzzing there—who knows?
She turned and fixed my red eye in her own. It's plain
I was her velvet-coated suitor, then. I interposed.
We left together. The room was hot and close.

## A Puzzle

*for R. J. Wedgwood*

Beautiful agnostic friend,
I found your jigsaw puzzle on the table,
the tumbled wreckage of a pastoral scene:
red of New England maples spilled, two broken silos—

time's fabled harvest and all labors' end.
I heard a cow low from her piece of green
and thought of hay that would be fitted into bales
bound for the barn you're raising chink by chink

beside the gabled farmhouse, where, to the unifying eye
of the mind, a woman stands at the sink,
musing on all it takes to keep a willful entropy at bay:
beds made, clothes washed, each daily surface swept

and put away. This she approves: beauty is order, she'll say,
and truth the lamp that switches on at dusk, restoring the colors
of the perishable day, through which, from time to time,
a hand-like shadow hesitates, then moves.

# The Wind Blows My Dictionary Open to "man"

Only it's not the definition—which casts off boldly:
*Bipedal primate mammal* . . . bright skiff on the epic sea—
but the illustrations on the facing page that stop me:

*Homo sapiens sapiens: Three Views.* Fig. 1 stands
contrapposto, robed in muscles, each with its numbered
dart. Flayed and pierced, he looks like a genial martyr,

left arm gesturing toward his posterior view (Fig. 2),
as if to say to the reader, who looks down from above,
"See, I am just as handsome from the back!" I run my finger

up the length of him, from the taut lyre-string of the *Achilles*,
to the *Long Adductor* of the thigh, to the *Superior Gracilis*
with its chaste omission, but he doesn't turn. He is gazing over

his right shoulder, into the orbital sockets of his skeleton self
(Fig. 3), two gentlemen of the world met here by chance, one
leaving the party just as this other, his late friend, is coming in.

He is, you can tell, a man of refined tastes, left *Ilium* raised
slightly, prehensile foot forward—a trim accountant
distinguished by *a notable development of the brain and resultant*

*capacity for abstract thought.* Time's man, his spine's a dry mast,
his limbs, freed shrouds that fixed him once between
the earth and heaven. What does he care now for the wind

that stirs the empty hold where the heart lived, though he recalls how, just yesterday, it whistled through his numbered days, filling them like sails.

## CRI DU COEUR

All night I have paced the floor with my colic heart,
      but it will not stop crying. I pick it up,

it wants to lie down. I lay it down; it demands
      to walk back and forth to the window.

I rock it. *Cry.* Swaddle it. *Cry.* Croon all the songs
      I know, *cry cry cry.* I whisper that it is mine,

that I would never harm it, but it will not do.
      It wants me to swear I'll never walk out the door

like a bad mother trailing smoke and perfume, never
      leave it alone in its barred crib, in the small

dark room, to wait through the interminable night,
      for an unimaginable morning.

# THE BRIDGE

*for Hal Simonson*

Before you could no longer lift your spoon,
but after you'd stopped counting the tumors,
cached in your chest like buried ordinance,
you fell out of bed, grazing the back of your hand.

Mornings and evenings you'd study the wound,
a skinless red square like a plot of land
seen from below clouds.

          Weeks before,
the receptionist at the dentist's office
had discreetly failed to schedule your next visit;
you'd let the magazines, the newspaper go,
but the skin kept doing the only thing it knew how—

each good cell continuing its blind
and earnest knitting, the gap narrowing
day by day from both sides, the way men
make a bridge over a bombed out river.

A satisfaction, you said at the end,
to know they'd succeeded,
the white scar sealed like an envelope
enclosing the order, the ambulance idling
at the water's edge.

## The Man from Eden

Pest Control Solutions is crouching in the bushes
of the Good Shepherd Cemetery. On his back,

the lethal canister, a slim proboscis in his gloved
left hand. Humped over in his brown uniform,

he looks like an avenging anteater, though it's not
ants he's after, but the eggs of the Canada Goose,

who has exceeded her quota. He does not think
about the Cosmic Egg of the Universe, yolk and white

of the material world, or this rustic emblem
of the Triune God, as he coats each shell with oil

and moves on. Outside, a quick anointing;
inside, a small setting sun. The Man from Eden

steps carefully around the pious increase of Adam
who wait, sealed and crated, for the crack

of the summoning horn, when they shall emerge
perfected; then, stumbling, wet, with still-blind eyes

flock sanctified into the New Jerusalem, that deathless town
that looks, for all we know, a lot like ours

on this ordinary evening—with spiders framed in their
rose windows, and the delicate hands of sewer rats

fine as El Greco saints', and, in the soft nimbus of
a street lamp, a host of termites, voracious with hosannas.

## Annunciation with Possum and Tomatoes

Faith, in spring, is a fertile bed, the hope of things
unseen—summer, round in the hand; toil, expectancy, ripe
weight. Grace, for a possum, is another thing:
a sleeping dog, an open gate, nine soft globes,

each bite, a new beginning. She ate them all,
but afterward I dreamed I saw a jungle of tomatoes
grown wild against the house, the fruit hanging fat, allegorical,
as the red canopy in Dieric Bouts's *Annunciation,*

in which the Virgin, surprised in her bedchamber,
looks up from her book, as the Flemish angel, plain
and reliable as a school nurse, calmly delivers the news.
His right finger points up at the Father,

or at the tomato-shaped folds of the drapery, as he explains
about the fruit of the womb, how it will ripen and spill
to repair the blight in the garden, the one that begot death
and beauty in turn, having first made thieves of us all.

Bouts's Holland would not taste tomatoes for another century;
the plague was swallowing citizens left and right,
but the good people of Haarlem still donned their peasant
leggings and took to the field. Perhaps the ploughman,

framed moments ago in the Gothic arch of the Virgin's window,
has set down his rake and is resting in the shade of a tree,

thinking about the fall and its hungers, and about himself,
kin to all mortal creatures, the ones who sow, and the ones

who plunder after them, who wake famished in the night,
all furred appetite, dreaming of a fruit they have never known:
flesh and seed, crotch and vine, its taste in the mouth sharp
as the known world, delectable as Eden.

## CARRIED AWAY

And when you *are,* you'll know it. First,
the musk of a summer night that slips
through your open window;
then pain at the scruff of the neck—
the hot mouth, rank and dripping. Next,
the labored passage through your own yard,
your face deep in moss and fern,
and the moment you tell yourself—
half-blind in the intoxicating air—
that *away* was your object, this *carrying* a gift
and benison, passage to an old belonging.

And later, by the strewn remnants
of the life before: a set of keys, a fragment
of tooth or bone, dropped in the soft
decaying leaves—the scented lap
of the world you *got*—
so much country you have never seen,
rough under your padded feet,
keen in your moon-colored eye.

## Aubade for Dave, the Electrician

Three mornings now you've had me
out of bed too early, a boy from White Center
with a tool belt and drop cloth.
Today you'll finish the complicated job,
and I know I'll miss you a little—
the coffee and idle talk,
the questions shouted from room
to room as I dress for work. And I'll miss
the enormous, tattooed snake
that coils around your arm and disappears
under your shirt sleeve,
the way it twists with your wrist
as you feed the long, black cables
into the narrow channel.

Once, at a county fair, I wore a king snake
on my skinny shoulders, its cool weight
heavy as a boy's arm, its tongue moving in
and out, like the tongue of the boy,
later, in my own mouth, and when
I imagine lying down with you,
something trips in the mind—
you *are* the boy, and we, twin filaments
coiled white and humming in that first
pure current of desire.

Three mornings now I've stood
in the darkened kitchen,
thinking about art and memory,
the fact and its mythic burden,
and now, before you go, I turn to you.
*Show me the rest of it* I say,
the words arcing in the space
between us—that hinged space that expands
to take in everything:
the snake and the serpent;
the man and the woman;
all the nights and days flowing forward
and back along the wire—
the moment you pull off your shirt
to show me; the hour I wake early
in the dark, remembering.

# Three

## Homeland Security

The bomb sniffing dog at the ferry terminal
is trying not to wag his tail,
but it's the Fourth of July—packs of kids
running wild over the hot asphalt;
ice cream cones topped with little
paper flags—

    and the dog, who knows
he's in over his head, keeps licking
the officer's finger as he points down
at the bumpers saying,
        *Focus, Rusty, focus.*

Not easy for one whose natural object
is always the readily digestible
to keep sticking his nose into
unlit corners—

    the very point of the author
of my book on contemporary poetry,
a man whose critiques roll like pulled grenades
into a crowded theater.

He thinks poets these days write
too much about dogs, which is true,
having bartered the choice thematic ordinance
of the literary canon for a fistful
of sparklers.

What's left, he asks,
but to *deflect*—to charm and obfuscate—
when the Sea of Faith bowed out
so long ago? Matthew Arnold,
crossing the wide water, heard it go—
the last sad slurp of an optimistic age.

Today in Pakistan,
a bomb went off at the market, killing
forty people and probably quite a few dogs,
and whatever each was thinking
in that swift and terrible crossing,
you can bet it wasn't about the Homeland,
or how art would redeem the shrill
waste of their lives. I like to think
each felt her shattered beauty rise
and, painless, fall back to the hand
that proffered it, as rain to the lap
of the sea. *Who wouldn't?*
Easy for me.

Stevens wanted words to comfort;
Berryman, to wound. We see them
standing on opposing shores,
fragrant with wood smoke
or strewn with bleaching bones.

Through the deep mid-channel,
the craft moves on,
helmed by circumstance,
past islands called for our lost tribes.

Volcanic,
good for picnics and burials,
dogs roam the margins of its tidal shoals,
and poets raise showers of sparks
to the night sky;
not stars, but true enough
to call them beautiful.

## SAUDADE

Whenever we listen to the loamy contralto
of Virginia Rodrigues, singing of blackness and exile

and the warm seas of Bahia, the neighbor's dog and I
stare at the speakers, full of sadness and desire.

Bruno is an Italian greyhound; we are mostly white;
we live in city apartments and do not speak Portuguese.

Still, something in the singer's ineluctable rhythms,
her long vowels like a beautiful howling, seems familiar,

and I know the way Bruno feels when I turn to address him,
his eyes fixed in anxious concentration, as though English

were a language he has inexplicably forgotten,
but will recover, as soon as he remembers how to fold

his long tongue into a ship that will ferry him out
of the taut wedge of a body in which he has been detained,

back to his native land. There, from the corporeal lap
of the sofa, whose back is the green coast of Salvadór,

whose arms, the beautiful, burdened arms of Africa,
he will reply, "Is the samba not proof that all possible

worlds are united in this one?" *Oh sim, certamente,*
I'll say, the music swelling around us like the slow

respiring sea, that is here and there, then and now,
and has been singing to everyone forever.

## Last Word

Forgetting you
is like forgetting a foreign language
I used to know by heart.

First to go,
the exotic moods
and tenses, meant to convey
the hypothetical future,
the conditional past.

Soon
articles slip away
from their gendered nouns,
and even the common irregulars
—*to have, to want*—
stop arriving on time
at the usual place,
where I wait

at the quiet table in the corner,
scanning the menu
for lost prepositions
—*above, between*—
still sweet on the tip
of the tongue;
rifling through

my sprung case of possessives
for—*What was the first word
you taught me?*

Two syllables,
soft as a breeze stirring
the curtains in a small hotel.
It started with s—
it meant "always."

## Sharing a Bath

On learning that film actress Veronica Lake
(1922–1973) once rented my apartment.


As I step into the cast iron tub,
first one foot, then the other, and ease into
the too-hot water, I think of you,
absent housemate, who stepped out

sixty years ago. Washed up
at twenty-five, a waitress at forty, your shine
brief as a soap bubble, who were you
but a hard luck story

worn to luster, frosty goddess
on a polar bear rug? There was the hair,
of course, blond drape that hid
your naked eye. You said

it did your acting for you
in films that promised love and trouble:
*Women Have Secrets, This Gun for Hire,
The Glass Key.* I think you were as fragile

as that, Veronica, shattered young
and ground into a thousand sequined shards
we're still finding in corners.
But tonight you're appearing

not as *The Blue Dahlia*,
flower that never was, or the icy moll,
dry as satin on some thug's arm,
but in *Apartment 112*,

posthumous role of a lifetime.
Veronica, pale perennial, step out
of that silk sarong, that soiled apron,
that winding sheet,

into the bath that is yours and mine.
Slip with me under the scented surface;
let our hair dark and light, entwine.
Adrift in our iron boat

we will wash one another, free
of the dust of the dead and the dust
of the living, talking of love and trouble
until the water cools

and the screen goes black
and the only star, framed in the window,
burns small and fair against the high
cold reel of heaven.

# Hoop Skirts Recalled

It's clear from her attitude of practiced ease,
that the woman, smiling out of the brochure
for Heritage Plantation Tours, relishes her role
as belle, though the effect is unconvincing.

Her too-perfect teeth might explain it,
or the way the shadows of the dark, muscled
oaks shading the big house behind her
fall so lightly on its broad staircase,

its open door. But it seems ungracious
to criticize when History's expecting us,
and when she's gone to such trouble
to get dressed: first the corset, all whalebones

and baffling hooks, then the hoop,
tied at the waist like an airy birdcage.
You have to hand it to dressmakers of old,
who understood better than we,

that impeding access only inflames desire,
a fact not mentioned in the brochure,
concerned, as it is, with the past's silhouette,
not its winnowing stays. Still,

I'd like to trade places with the Heritage Girl,
to sink on my skirts like a pebble, dropped
in a pond, the waves rippling out
to these strangers, who have gathered

on the lawn in shorts and flip flops, waiting
for entry. Like her, I would keep my own
counsel, knowing that if history's a line,
the past is all circumference,

in whose voluminous folds a small brown
wren abides at the crux of two limbs,
her call now soft, now shrill,
under the brocaded dome of the sky.

## RUMMAGE SALE

Forgive me, Aunt Phyllis, for rejecting the cut
glass dishes—the odd set you gathered piece
by piece from thirteen boxes of Lux laundry soap.

Pardon me, eggbeater, for preferring the whisk;
and you, small ship in a bottle, for the diminutive
size of your ocean. Please don't tell my mother,

hideous lamp, that the light you provided
was never enough. Domestic deities, do not be angry
that my counters are not white with flour;

no one is sorrier than I, iron skillet, for the heavy
longing for lightness directing my mortal hand.
And my apologies, to you, above all,

forsaken dresses, that sway from a rod between
ladders behind me, clicking your plastic tongues
at the girl you once made beautiful,

and the woman, with a hard heart and
softening body, who stands in the driveway
making change.

## Haute Couture

Just when you think it can't be mended,
the April sky,
dingy from over-washing,
gray hem of clouds coming down,
they arrive—
the assiduous tailors,
with their blue smocks,
their scissortails.

Then you step out of winter like a grave
and awkward garment,
happy beyond measure to know
that from this same bolt of blue
they clothed the pharaohs,
an Etruscan woman scaling a fish,
even your elderly neighbors,
sitting together
with their oxygen canisters
at the edge of the lawn,

May slipping softly
down over their shoulders,
as in the old stories
where the blind see,
the beggar walks in robes of gold,
and everyone is saved.

## WISHBONE

Tonight across America, in the swank salons
of Midtown matriarchs, in the steaming kitchens
of the Great Plains, people are gathering

to break the forked clavicles of domestic fowl.
The winner gets the wish, as we all know—
but from whom? Not the bird, surely,

who probably still bears a grudge, or Jesus,
that stray bachelor who turns up year after year.
More likely some stone-faced, runic deity,

and this, his last grave office. Solemn, invisible,
he waits by the fire, dismayed that the squalling
two-year-old in the small, high throne shall not

be sacrificed for the good of all, yet pleased
that the contest lives on, with its instrument
so little changed: two arms, joined

like a compass; the Wish sparking in the field
of its circumference, waiting for the snap.
From age to circling age we've played—

Shirts against Bones, opponents in this game
whose odds our side's forgotten, though the stakes
haven't changed: long life and the wolf at bay.

And how lucky we are to have won this round,
to be here waiting for pie, while the loser
has to be the bone, cramped in some marble

vault, or nowhere at all—a skein of ashes
unspooled in the air. And what wouldn't he give
to be here among us, bored and sated,

watching the candle grow short in its silver cup,
and the dog, tracing her gentle arc under the table,
moving from hand to hand.

# A True Story

An old man was dying in the hospital,
    my friend the doctor told me.

He was 89, his whole life a tailor in a shop
    below the room where he was born.

He had no one, so a kind aid from Ghana
    sat with him, one hand in his,

the other holding her sandwich. The waves
    on the monitor slowed. His heart

was a small red boat on the long tide,
    going out. At the end he opened

his eyes. *Cool air, Cool air,* he said, and because
    it was the 12th floor, the windows sealed,

the aid leans over and exhales softly on the top
    of his head, to ruffle his hair a bit,

and they stay like that for a few minutes until
    he dies, his face turned to the breeze.

That was a long time ago. My friend is gone;
    the hospital's become a vacant lot.

Some nights I wake with those words in my ear,
  unsure if they're the plea of the old Jew

or the answering breath of the African woman,
  or the beautiful lie that binds them

like a dart and a seam; the cold clarity of glass
  and the wide blue draft beyond.

## A Little Dream of You

How difficult to rise and face the day
when I have just spent the night with the handsome
author of the book I'm reading on Italy, whose face,
superimposed on the cover, hangs in the evening sky
over the *cittadella* like a collective sigh.
Eight hours ago we hardly knew each other,

though I was thinking, as I turned out the light,
that reading his chapter on the happy island of Parma
put me in mind of an Italian movie, in which a shy
village girl watches from the shore as her love
unloads his catch of the true and the beautiful
as the old ones look on admiringly, mending their nets.

Just how we arrived at the noisy restaurant
where we dined last night with his mother is unclear,
though I recall how the delicate web of her shawl
caught on my watch and dissolved into sea foam in my hands,
while the Italian girlfriend, his reason for coming to Italy
we learn in the preface, laughed nearby. Too bad for her,

by the time the mayor arrived with a plate
of sardines, my dress lay under the table like a cat
coiled in sleep—another faux pas, I realize now—
though my author's lips, brushing the hair from my neck
as I leaned back in his arms, were as light as the breeze
of a fan purring in the summer dawn.

I may never know for certain who pulled the fire alarm
that snatched me away at 7:15, stranding me here
on the narrow sandbar of my bed, unable to explain.
I like to think he waited awhile outside the restaurant
and then walked sadly home, finding no warmth
in the ochre faces of the flats he loves,

knowing that when we meet again he'll be strolling
arm in arm with another, and I, with the one
I'm reading now. We'll nod discretely as we take our turn
around the great fountain, as one turns the page of the day,
and the night comes on, and we close the book
and lay it down beside us.

## Acknowledgments

My thanks are due to the editors of the following publications, in which some of these poems first appeared:

*Christianity and Literature*: "The Man from Eden"; *IMAGE*: "A True Story"; *New Letters*: "Hangman" and "A Puzzle"; *Sewanee Theological Review*: "Annunciation with Possum and Tomatoes"; *Smartish Pace*: "Last Word" and "Haute Couture"; *Southern Poetry Review*: "Your Life in Dances" and "A Little Dream of You"; *Poetry Society of America*: "Fly."

I am also grateful for grants and fellowships from Seattle Pacific University and the Sewanee Writers' Conference, whose support has helped greatly in the completion of this book. Finally, I'd like to thank the many friends and colleagues who've offered advice and encouragement along the way, among them, John Hollander, Charles Martin, Greg Williamson, Phillis Levin, Wyatt Prunty, David Barber, Greg Wolfe, Harold Simonson, James Fritz, and Madeline DeFrees, who continues to challenge and inspire.